MASTERING OPTIONS

A Comprehensive Guide to Profitable Trading

Strategies

by

Lalit Mohanty

Table of Contents

Introduction: Unlocking the Power of Options Trading

Chapter 1: **Understanding Options Basics**

- The fundamentals of options: calls and puts
- Option pricing and the Greeks (Delta, Gamma, Theta, Vega)
- In-the-money, at-the-money, and out-of-the-money options

Chapter 2: **Long Call Strategy: Riding the Bull**

- How to use long call options for bullish market expectations
- Risk and reward analysis
- Selecting the right strike price and expiration date

Chapter 3: **Long Put Strategy: Profiting from the Bear**

- Utilizing long put options for bearish market predictions
- Managing risk through position sizing and timing
- Choosing the appropriate strike price and expiration date

Chapter 4: **Covered Call Strategy: Income Generation with Safety Nets**

- Writing covered calls to generate income

- Balancing risk and return

- Adjusting positions based on market conditions

Chapter 5: **Protective Put Strategy: Safeguarding Your Investments**

- Hedging with protective puts to limit downside risk

- Building a protective put strategy around existing stock positions

- Practical examples and case studies

Chapter 6: **Long Straddle Strategy: Profiting from Market Volatility**

- Employing long straddles to capitalize on price volatility

- Calculating breakeven points and potential gains

- Adjusting the strategy for changing market conditions

Chapter 7: **Credit Spread Strategy: Time Decay for Income**

- Creating credit spreads to take advantage of time decay

- Balancing risk and reward in credit spread positions

- Adjusting positions as expiration approaches

Chapter 8: **Iron Condor Strategy: Navigating Sideways Markets**

- Constructing iron condors to profit in range-bound markets

- Managing risk through proper position sizing and adjustment techniques

- Real-world examples of successful iron condor trades

Chapter 9: **Butterfly Spread Strategy: Capitalizing on Low Volatility**

- Utilizing butterfly spreads for low volatility environments

- Adjusting the strategy for different market conditions

- Risk management and profit potential in butterfly spreads

Chapter 10: **Ratio Spread Strategy: Leveraging Risk and Reward**

- Implementing ratio spreads for asymmetric risk-reward profiles

- Selecting the right ratio for specific market expectations

- Dynamic adjustments to optimize the strategy's performance

Conclusion: Crafting Your Options Trading Journey

Appendix: **Advanced Concepts and Strategies**

- Exploring advanced options strategies
- Using options in conjunction with other financial instruments
- Risk management techniques for advanced traders

Glossary

- Key terms and definitions for quick reference

Resources

- Additional reading, online courses, and tools for further learning

PREFACE

This book provides a comprehensive guide to understanding and implementing various option trading strategies, catering to both novice and experienced traders. Each chapter is designed to equip readers with the knowledge and skills needed to navigate different market conditions and enhance their proficiency in options trading.

INTRODUCTION

UNLOCKING THE POWER OF OPTIONS TRADING

Welcome to the exciting world of options trading, a dynamic financial landscape where strategic decision-making and precise execution can lead to substantial profits. In this introductory chapter, we embark on a journey to unlock the power of options trading—a realm that offers unique opportunities for investors to manage risk, generate income, and capitalize on market movements.

The Evolution of Options Trading

Options trading has come a long way since its inception centuries ago. Originally designed as risk management tools for agricultural commodities, options have evolved into sophisticated financial instruments that play a crucial role in modern financial markets. Today, options are traded on various assets, including stocks, indices, and commodities, providing traders with a versatile toolkit to navigate an ever-changing market environment.

Why Options Trading?

Options trading offers distinct advantages that set it apart from traditional forms of investing. Unlike buying or selling stocks outright, options provide flexibility, enabling traders to profit in both rising and falling markets. By understanding and implementing various options strategies, investors can tailor their approach to market conditions, making it a valuable tool for both conservative and speculative trading styles.

Unlocking Potential with Limited Risk

One of the key attractions of options trading is the ability to achieve significant returns with a predefined and limited risk. Options strategies allow traders to construct positions that align with their market outlook while effectively managing the downside. This risk-management feature empowers traders to participate in the market with confidence, even in times of heightened volatility.

Harnessing the Greeks: A Precision Toolset

To truly unlock the power of options trading, one must grasp the intricacies of the Greeks—Delta, Gamma, Theta, and Vega. These parameters provide insights into how option prices are influenced by changes in stock prices, time decay, and volatility. Armed with this knowledge, traders can fine-tune their strategies and optimize their positions for maximum effectiveness.

Your Guide to Success

This book serves as your comprehensive guide to mastering options trading strategies. Each chapter delves into a specific strategy, offering a detailed exploration of its mechanics, risk and reward dynamics, and practical implementation. Whether you are a novice trader looking to build a solid foundation or an experienced investor seeking to refine your skills, this guide is tailored to meet your needs.

Prepare to explore the potential of long calls and puts, covered calls, protective puts, and advanced strategies like iron condors and butterfly spreads. As we navigate through these chapters, you'll gain the knowledge and confidence to leverage options effectively, making informed decisions that align with your financial goals.

Get ready to unlock the power of options trading and embark on a journey that can transform the way you approach the financial markets. The tools are in your hands—let's embark on this exciting adventure together.

CHAPTER 1

UNDERSTANDING OPTIONS BASICS

Welcome to the foundation of options trading—the realm where financial flexibility and strategic foresight converge. In this chapter, we will unravel the fundamentals of options, exploring the two primary building blocks: calls and puts. Additionally, we'll delve into the critical concepts of option pricing and the Greeks—Delta, Gamma, Theta, and Vega. Finally, we'll demystify the classification of options into in-the-money, at-the-money, and out-of-the-money, laying the groundwork for your journey into the dynamic world of options trading.

1.1 Calls and Puts: The Cornerstones of Options

Options, at their core, are financial instruments that give investors the right, but not the obligation, to buy (call option) or sell (put option) an underlying asset at a predetermined price, known as the strike price, within a specified period, known as the expiration date. Let's break down the two primary types of options:

1.1.1 Call Options: Riding the Upside

- A call option provides the holder with the right to buy the underlying asset at the specified strike price.

- Call buyers anticipate that the value of the underlying asset will rise, allowing them to purchase at a lower price and potentially profit from the upward movement.

1.1.2 Put Options: Profiting from the Downside

- A put option grants the holder the right to sell the underlying asset at the predetermined strike price.

- Put buyers aim to profit from a decline in the value of the underlying asset, allowing them to sell at a higher strike price, regardless of the market price.

1.2 Option Pricing and the Greeks: Understanding the Dynamics

Understanding how options are priced is crucial for effective trading. The Black-Scholes model, among others, is commonly used to calculate option prices. Within this pricing framework, the Greeks play a vital role:

1.2.1 Delta: Sensitivity to Price Changes

- Delta measures the change in the option's price concerning a one-point movement in the underlying asset's price.

- For call options, delta values range from 0 to 1, indicating the probability of the option expiring in-the-money. For put options, delta values range from -1 to 0, representing the probability of the option finishing in-the-money.

1.2.2 Gamma: Rate of Change of Delta

- Gamma assesses how much the delta of an option changes with a one-point move in the underlying asset.

- Gamma is crucial for understanding how delta may change as the underlying asset's price fluctuates.

1.2.3 Theta: Time Decay Factor

- Theta measures the rate of time decay in an option's price as the expiration date approaches.

- It highlights the impact of time on the option's value, with options losing value as they approach expiration.

1.2.4 Vega: Sensitivity to Volatility Changes

- Vega gauges how much an option's price changes concerning a 1% shift in implied volatility.

- Traders use vega to understand how sensitive an option is to changes in market volatility.

1.3 In-the-Money, At-the-Money, and Out-of-the-Money Options

Options are classified based on their relationship to the current market price of the underlying asset:

1.3.1 In-the-Money (ITM) Options

- For call options, ITM means the stock price is above the strike price.

- For put options, ITM indicates the stock price is below the strike price.

- ITM options generally have intrinsic value.

1.3.2 At-the-Money (ATM) Options

- The strike price of the option is approximately equal to the current market price of the underlying asset.

- ATM options typically have higher time value.

1.3.3 Out-of-the-Money (OTM) Options

- For call options, OTM means the stock price is below the strike price.

- For put options, OTM indicates the stock price is above the strike price.

- OTM options generally consist solely of time value.

Understanding the distinctions between these classifications is essential for crafting effective options trading strategies tailored to different market conditions.

In this chapter, we've laid the groundwork for your exploration into the world of options trading. Armed with an understanding of calls and puts, option pricing, the Greeks, and option classifications, you are now better equipped to navigate the subsequent chapters, where we'll delve deeper into specific strategies that leverage these fundamental concepts. As you continue your journey, remember: knowledge is your greatest asset in the realm of options trading.

CHAPTER 2

LONG CALL STRATEGY: RIDING THE BULL

In this chapter, we'll explore the Long Call strategy, a powerful tool in your options trading arsenal when anticipating upward market movements. By the end of this chapter, you'll understand how to implement a Long Call strategy, assess its risks and rewards, and make informed decisions when selecting the optimal strike price and expiration date.

2.1 The Long Call Strategy: Unleashing Bullish Potential

The Long Call strategy is a straightforward and bullish approach to options trading. It involves buying call options with the expectation that the price of the underlying asset will rise. Here's how it works:

2.1.1 Buying Call Options

- When you buy a call option, you acquire the right to purchase the underlying asset at a predetermined price (strike price) before or at the expiration date.

- This strategy allows you to participate in the potential upside of the underlying asset with a limited initial investment.

2.1.2 Market Expectations

- The Long Call strategy thrives in bullish market conditions, where you anticipate the price of the underlying asset to increase.

- As the asset's price rises, the value of your call option increases, allowing you to sell it at a profit or exercise the option to buy the underlying asset at a lower, predetermined price.

2.2 Risk and Reward Analysis: Navigating the Upside Potential

Every trading strategy comes with its own set of risks and rewards. Let's examine the risk and reward profile of the Long Call strategy:

2.2.1 Potential Losses

- The maximum risk in a Long Call strategy is limited to the premium paid for the call option.

- If the price of the underlying asset doesn't rise as expected, the call option may expire worthless, and you lose the initial investment.

2.2.2 Unlimited Profit Potential

- The profit potential in a Long Call strategy is theoretically unlimited.

- As the price of the underlying asset rises, the call option's value increases. There is no cap on the profit you can realize from a rising market.

2.3 Selecting the Right Strike Price: Precision in Bullish Anticipation

Choosing the right strike price is a critical aspect of the Long Call strategy. Here are considerations to guide your decision:

2.3.1 In-the-Money (ITM) vs. Out-of-the-Money (OTM)

- ITM call options have a higher initial cost but offer more intrinsic value.

- OTM call options are cheaper but rely heavily on the underlying asset's price surpassing the strike price for profitability.

2.3.2 Strike Price and Upside Potential

- Select a strike price that aligns with your bullish expectations.

- A lower strike price offers a higher chance of profitability but comes with a higher initial cost.

2.4 Choosing the Optimal Expiration Date: Balancing Time and Risk

The expiration date of the call option plays a crucial role in the success of the Long Call strategy. Consider the following factors:

2.4.1 Time Decay (Theta)

- Longer-dated options provide more time for the underlying asset to move in the desired direction.

- However, time decay accelerates as expiration approaches, impacting the option's value.

2.4.2 Balancing Risk and Time Horizon

- Align the expiration date with your time horizon for the bullish move.

- Shorter-term options may be suitable for rapid price movements, while longer-term options provide more flexibility but expose you to increased time decay.

2.5 Realizing Profits: Knowing When to Exit

Successfully riding the bull requires an exit strategy. Consider the following approaches:

2.5.1 Setting Price Targets

- Define profit targets based on technical analysis or predetermined percentage gains.

- Lock in profits by selling the call option or exercising it to buy the underlying asset at a lower price.

2.5.2 Managing Losses

- Implement stop-loss orders to limit potential losses.

- Be disciplined in cutting losses if the market doesn't move as anticipated.

CHAPTER 3

LONG PUT STRATEGY: PROFITING FROM THE BEAR

In this chapter, we'll explore how to harness the power of long put options to capitalize on downward market movements. By the end of this chapter, you'll gain insights into effectively implementing a Long Put strategy, managing risk through position sizing and timing, and making informed decisions when selecting the optimal strike price and expiration date.

3.1 The Long Put Strategy: A Bear's Arsenal

The Long Put strategy is a bearish approach to options trading, designed to profit from a decline in the price of the underlying asset. Let's delve into the key components of this strategy:

3.1.1 Buying Put Options

- When you buy a put option, you secure the right to sell the underlying asset at a predetermined price (strike price) before or at the expiration date.

- This strategy allows you to profit from a falling market without the need to short-sell the underlying asset.

3.1.2 Ideal Market Conditions

- The Long Put strategy thrives in bearish market conditions, where you anticipate the price of the underlying asset to decrease.

- As the asset's price falls, the value of your put option increases, enabling you to sell it at a profit or exercise the option to sell the underlying asset at a higher, predetermined price.

3.2 Managing Risk: A Paramount Consideration

While the Long Put strategy presents an opportunity for significant profits in a bearish market, prudent risk management is essential. Let's explore ways to manage risk through position sizing and timing:

3.2.1 Position Sizing

- Determine the appropriate size of your put option position based on your risk tolerance and overall portfolio strategy.

- Avoid overexposure to a single trade by diversifying your options positions.

3.2.2 Timing is Key

- Anticipating the timing of a bearish move is crucial for the success of the Long Put strategy.

- Use technical analysis, market indicators, and other tools to enhance your timing accuracy.

3.3 Choosing the Appropriate Strike Price: Precision in Bearish Expectations

Selecting the right strike price is a critical aspect of the Long Put strategy. Here are key considerations to guide your decision:

3.3.1 In-the-Money (ITM) vs. Out-of-the-Money (OTM) Puts

- ITM put options have higher initial costs but offer more intrinsic value.

- OTM put options are less expensive but rely heavily on the underlying asset's price falling below the strike price for profitability.

3.3.2 Strike Price and Downside Potential

- Choose a strike price that aligns with your bearish expectations.

- A lower strike price increases the likelihood of profitability but comes with a higher initial cost.

3.4 Selecting the Optimal Expiration Date: Balancing Time and Risk

Just like with the Long Call strategy, the expiration date of the put option is a crucial factor. Consider the following:

3.4.1 Time Decay (Theta)

- Longer-dated options provide more time for the underlying asset to move in the anticipated direction.

- However, time decay accelerates as expiration approaches, impacting the option's value.

3.4.2 Aligning with Your Time Horizon

- Match the expiration date with your expected timeframe for the bearish move.

- Shorter-term options may be suitable for rapid price movements, while longer-term options provide more flexibility at the cost of increased time decay.

3.5 Realizing Profits: Exit Strategies in a Bearish Landscape

Successfully navigating the bearish terrain requires a sound exit strategy. Consider the following approaches:

3.5.1 Setting Profit Targets

- Define profit targets based on technical analysis or predetermined percentage gains.

- Lock in profits by selling the put option or exercising it to sell the underlying asset at a higher, predetermined price.

3.5.2 Managing Losses

- Implement stop-loss orders to limit potential losses.

- Be disciplined in cutting losses if the market doesn't move as expected.

CHAPTER 4

COVERED CALL STRATEGY: INCOME GENERATION WITH SAFETY NETS

In this chapter, we'll explore how to leverage the Covered Call strategy to generate income while adding a layer of protection to your portfolio. By the end of this chapter, you'll understand how to write covered calls, balance risk and return, and make informed adjustments to your positions based on evolving market conditions.

4.1 The Covered Call Strategy: An Overview

The Covered Call strategy is a popular and conservative options strategy employed by income-seeking investors. It involves the simultaneous purchase of an underlying asset (usually stocks) and the sale of call options against that asset. Here's how it works:

4.1.1 Buying the Underlying Asset

- Start by purchasing shares of a stock you believe will remain relatively stable or experience only modest price increases.

4.1.2 Selling Call Options

- Simultaneously, sell call options against the shares you own. Each call option represents the right, but not the obligation, for the buyer to purchase your shares at a predetermined price (strike price) before or at the expiration date.

4.1.3 Generating Income

- By selling call options, you collect premiums, generating a consistent income stream.

4.2 Balancing Risk and Return: The Key to Covered Calls

The Covered Call strategy offers a balanced approach to options trading, combining income generation with risk mitigation. Let's explore the risk and return dynamics:

4.2.1 Limited Upside Potential

- The maximum profit in a Covered Call strategy is capped at the sum of the premium collected and any capital gains in the stock's price up to the strike price.

4.2.2 Downside Protection

- The ownership of the underlying stock provides a safety net. If the stock price falls, the premium collected from selling the call options cushions the potential losses.

4.2.3 Consistent Income

- Covered Calls generate a steady income through the premiums received from selling call options. This income can be particularly attractive in sideways or slightly bullish markets.

4.3 Adjusting Positions: Adapting to Market Conditions

Successful implementation of the Covered Call strategy involves adapting to changing market conditions. Consider the following adjustments:

4.3.1 Rolling Options

- As expiration dates approach, consider "rolling" options by buying back the current options and selling new ones with a later expiration date. This allows you to capture additional premiums.

4.3.2 Managing Underlying Stock Position

- If the stock experiences a significant price increase, you may choose to sell it and realize capital gains. Alternatively, you can buy back the call options to free up the stock for potential further appreciation.

4.3.3 Market Volatility Considerations

- During periods of heightened volatility, evaluate the strike prices and expiration dates to ensure they align with your risk tolerance and market outlook.

CHAPTER 5

PROTECTIVE PUT STRATEGY: SAFEGUARDING YOUR INVESTMENTS

In the unpredictable landscape of financial markets, protecting your investments from potential downturns is a critical aspect of risk management. The Protective Put strategy is a powerful tool designed to serve as a safety net for your portfolio, allowing you to limit downside risk while maintaining exposure to potential gains. In this chapter, we'll explore the mechanics of hedging with protective puts, building a strategy around existing stock positions, and reinforce these concepts with practical examples and case studies.

5.1 The Protective Put Strategy: A Hedge Against Downside Risk

The Protective Put strategy, also known as the "married put," involves purchasing a put option for each share of a stock you own. This strategy serves as a form of insurance against potential declines in the stock's price.

5.1.1 Buying Put Options for Protection

- For each share of stock you own, buy a put option with a strike price and expiration date that aligns with your risk tolerance and investment horizon.

- This put option acts as a form of insurance, allowing you to sell the stock at the strike price, limiting potential losses.

5.1.2 Maintaining Stock Exposure

- Unlike selling the stock outright, the Protective Put strategy enables you to maintain your stock position, participating in any potential upside while having downside protection.

5.2 Building a Protective Put Strategy: Tailoring to Your Portfolio

Implementing a Protective Put strategy involves thoughtful consideration of your existing stock positions and risk tolerance. Let's explore the key components:

5.2.1 Identifying Stocks for Protection

- Evaluate your portfolio and identify stocks that you wish to protect against potential downside risk.

- Consider the historical volatility of each stock and its susceptibility to market fluctuations.

5.2.2 Selecting Strike Prices and Expiration Dates

- Choose put options with strike prices that align with your acceptable level of risk.

- Opt for expiration dates that provide sufficient coverage for the anticipated time frame of potential market volatility.

5.2.3 Calculating Cost of Protection

- Understand the cost of implementing the Protective Put strategy, factoring in the premiums paid for the put options.

- Evaluate whether the cost is justified by the level of protection it provides.

5.3 Practical Examples: Applying Protective Puts in Real Scenarios

Let's walk through practical examples to illustrate how the Protective Put strategy works in real-life situations:

5.3.1 Example 1: Hedging a High-Volatility Stock

- Explore a scenario where a high-volatility stock is part of your portfolio, and you decide to use protective puts to limit potential losses.

5.3.2 Example 2: Safeguarding Profits

- Consider a situation where you've experienced significant gains in a particular stock and wish to safeguard those profits against a potential market downturn.

5.4 Case Studies: Learning from Real-world Implementations

We'll delve into case studies that showcase the Protective Put strategy in action, examining how it has been utilized in different market conditions to protect investments and manage risk.

5.4.1 Case Study 1: Mitigating Downside Risk in a Bear Market

- Explore a case study where the Protective Put strategy proves effective in mitigating losses during a bear market.

5.4.2 Case Study 2: Enhancing Risk-Adjusted Returns

- Analyze a case study demonstrating how the Protective Put strategy enhances risk-adjusted returns in a volatile market environment.

5.5 Tips and Considerations: Enhancing Your Protective Put Strategy

As you navigate the Protective Put strategy, consider the following tips and additional considerations to optimize your approach:

5.5.1 Monitoring and Adjusting Positions

- Regularly assess your portfolio and adjust the protective put positions based on changes in market conditions and your investment objectives.

5.5.2 Combining with Other Risk Management Techniques

- Explore how the Protective Put strategy can complement other risk management techniques, such as diversification and stop-loss orders.

CHAPTER 6

LONG STRADDLE STRATEGY: PROFITING FROM MARKET VOLATILITY

In the dynamic and ever-changing landscape of financial markets, volatility presents both challenges and opportunities. The Long Straddle strategy is a versatile approach that allows traders to capitalize on significant price movements, regardless of whether they are up or down. In this chapter, we'll explore how to effectively employ Long Straddles to profit from market volatility. We'll delve into the calculation of breakeven points, potential gains, and provide insights on adjusting the strategy to navigate changing market conditions.

6.1 The Long Straddle Strategy: A Play on Volatility

The Long Straddle strategy involves simultaneously purchasing a call option and a put option with the same strike price and expiration date. This strategy is employed when the trader anticipates a substantial price movement in the underlying asset but is uncertain about the direction of the move.

6.1.1 Buying a Call Option

- The call option allows the trader to profit from upward price movements.

6.1.2 Buying a Put Option

- The put option enables the trader to profit from downward price movements.

6.1.3 Capitalizing on Volatility

- The Long Straddle strategy profits from volatility by generating gains as the price of the underlying asset makes significant moves in either direction.

6.2 Calculating Breakeven Points: The Key Metrics

Understanding the breakeven points is crucial for managing the Long Straddle strategy effectively. Let's explore how to calculate them:

6.2.1 Upper Breakeven Point

- The upper breakeven point is the price at which gains from the call option offset the combined cost of the call and put options.

6.2.2 Lower Breakeven Point

- The lower breakeven point is the price at which gains from the put option offset the combined cost of the call and put options.

6.3 Potential Gains: Profiting from Significant Moves

The Long Straddle strategy offers unlimited profit potential if the underlying asset experiences a substantial price movement. Let's examine how potential gains are determined:

6.3.1 Profit from Call Option

- Gains from the call option increase as the price of the underlying asset rises.

6.3.2 Profit from Put Option

- Gains from the put option increase as the price of the underlying asset falls.

6.3.3 Total Potential Gains

- The total potential gains are the sum of profits from both the call and put options.

6.4 Adjusting the Strategy: Navigating Changing Market Conditions

The effectiveness of the Long Straddle strategy depends on the market's response to volatility. Consider the following adjustments to optimize the strategy:

6.4.1 Early Closure

- If the underlying asset experiences a significant price movement early in the trade, consider closing the position to lock in profits.

6.4.2 Rolling Options

- If the price movement is gradual or not as anticipated, explore the possibility of rolling the options to extend the timeframe and capture additional gains.

6.4.3 Hedging with Additional Options

- In response to changing market conditions, consider incorporating additional options to hedge against adverse price movements and manage risk.

CHAPTER 7

CREDIT SPREAD STRATEGY: TIME DECAY FOR INCOME

In this chapter, we'll explore how to create credit spreads to capitalize on time decay, balancing risk and reward in credit spread positions. As we delve into the mechanics of this strategy, we'll also discuss essential considerations for adjusting positions as expiration approaches.

7.1 The Credit Spread Strategy: An Overview

The Credit Spread strategy involves simultaneously selling and buying options to create a net credit. Typically, this strategy is implemented when the trader anticipates minimal price movement in the underlying asset. The goal is to profit from time decay and generate income through the premiums collected.

7.1.1 Selling a Higher-Priced Option (Credit Leg)

- The trader sells an option with a higher premium, known as the "credit leg." This option benefits from time decay as it loses value over time.

7.1.2 Buying a Lower-Priced Option (Debit Leg)

- To limit potential losses, the trader simultaneously buys an option with a lower premium, known as the "debit leg."

7.1.3 Net Credit and Maximum Loss

- The difference in premiums between the credit and debit legs results in a net credit, which is the maximum potential profit. The maximum loss is limited to the difference in strike prices minus the net credit.

7.2 Balancing Risk and Reward: Essential Considerations

To effectively implement the Credit Spread strategy, it's crucial to strike a balance between risk and reward. Let's explore key considerations:

7.2.1 Selecting Strike Prices

- Choose strike prices based on your assessment of the underlying asset's price movement. Wider spreads provide higher credits but also increase potential risk.

7.2.2 Evaluating Risk-Reward Ratio

- Assess the risk-reward ratio to ensure that the potential reward justifies the risk. A favorable risk-reward ratio is a cornerstone of successful credit spread positions.

7.2.3 Managing Position Size

- Consider the overall portfolio and position size to avoid overexposure to a single trade. Diversifying credit spread positions across different assets can help manage risk.

7.3 Adjusting Positions as Expiration Approaches

As expiration approaches, adjustments may be necessary to optimize the Credit Spread strategy. Consider the following approaches:

7.3.1 Closing Positions Early

- If the trade is profitable or there's a significant portion of the premium realized, consider closing the position before expiration to capture gains and reduce risk.

7.3.2 Rolling Positions

- Extend the duration of the credit spread by rolling the options to a later expiration date. This strategy allows for additional time decay and potential adjustments to strike prices.

7.3.3 Unwinding Losing Positions

- If the trade is moving against you, evaluate whether it makes sense to unwind the position to limit losses. This may involve closing both legs of the credit spread.

CHAPTER 8

IRON CONDOR STRATEGY: NAVIGATING SIDEWAYS MARKETS

In this chapter, we will explore the construction of Iron Condors to profit from sideways movements, delve into risk management through position sizing and adjustment techniques, and provide real-world examples of successful Iron Condor trades.

8.1 The Iron Condor Strategy: An Overview

The Iron Condor strategy is designed for markets with low volatility and minimal directional movement. It involves simultaneously selling an out-of-the-money (OTM) put spread and an OTM call spread, creating a range-bound profit zone.

8.1.1 Selling a Put Spread (Bull Put Spread)

- The trader sells an OTM put option while simultaneously buying a lower strike put option, creating a bullish position with limited risk.

8.1.2 Selling a Call Spread (Bear Call Spread)

- Simultaneously, the trader sells an OTM call option while buying a higher strike call option, creating a bearish position with limited risk.

8.1.3 Profit Zone and Maximum Loss

- The combined effect of the put and call spreads creates a profit zone between the two strike prices. The maximum loss is limited to the difference in strike prices minus the net credit received.

8.2 Managing Risk: Position Sizing and Adjustment Techniques

Effectively managing risk is crucial when implementing the Iron Condor strategy. Consider the following techniques:

8.2.1 Proper Position Sizing

- Determine the appropriate size of the Iron Condor position based on your risk tolerance and overall portfolio strategy. Avoid overcommitting to a single trade.

8.2.2 Adjustment Techniques

- If the market moves against the Iron Condor position, consider adjustment techniques such as rolling the position to different strike prices or expiration dates to mitigate potential losses.

8.2.3 Early Closure

- If a substantial portion of the premium is realized or the market is showing signs of unfavorable movement, consider closing the Iron Condor position early to lock in profits and reduce risk.

8.3 Real-world Examples: Successful Iron Condor Trades

To illustrate the effectiveness of the Iron Condor strategy, let's explore real-world examples of successful trades in different market scenarios:

8.3.1 Example 1: Profiting in a Sideways Market

- Explore a scenario where the market remains range-bound, allowing the Iron Condor strategy to generate consistent profits.

8.3.2 Example 2: Adapting to Changing Volatility

- Examine a situation where the trader adjusts the Iron Condor position to navigate changing market volatility, showcasing the strategy's adaptability.

8.4 Case Studies: Navigating Iron Condor Trades

Delve into case studies that demonstrate the implementation, management, and potential outcomes of Iron Condor trades in various market conditions:

8.4.1 Case Study 1: A Successful Iron Condor in Low Volatility

- Analyze a case study where an Iron Condor position thrives in a low-volatility environment, capitalizing on the strategy's suitability for such market conditions.

8.4.2 Case Study 2: Adapting to a Trending Market

- Explore a case study where the trader adjusts the Iron Condor to navigate a trending market, showcasing the strategy's flexibility.

8.5 Tips for Success: Enhancing Your Iron Condor Strategy

As you navigate the Iron Condor strategy, consider the following tips to optimize your approach:

8.5.1 Monitoring Economic Events

- Stay informed about economic events and market indicators that may impact volatility and adjust your Iron Condor positions accordingly.

8.5.2 Regular Portfolio Review

- Conduct regular reviews of your overall portfolio to ensure that Iron Condor positions align with your risk tolerance and market outlook.

CHAPTER 9

BUTTERFLY SPREAD STRATEGY: CAPITALIZING ON LOW VOLATILITY

In this chapter, we'll explore the intricacies of utilizing Butterfly Spreads, adjust the strategy for different market conditions, and delve into the crucial aspects of risk management and profit potential inherent in butterfly spreads.

9.1 The Butterfly Spread Strategy: An Overview

The Butterfly Spread strategy is a neutral options trading strategy designed to capitalize on low volatility. It involves the simultaneous purchase and sale of three options at the same expiration date but with different strike prices. Let's break down the components of a Butterfly Spread:

9.1.1 Central Strike Price (Long Call/Put)

- Buy one option with a central strike price, which serves as the focal point of the butterfly.

9.1.2 Higher and Lower Strike Prices (Short Calls/Puts)

- Sell two options, one with a higher strike price and one with a lower strike price.

9.1.3 Net Debit and Profit Potential

- The strategy typically involves a net debit, and the maximum profit is achieved if the underlying asset closes at the central strike price at expiration.

9.2 Adjusting the Strategy for Different Market Conditions

Effectively implementing the Butterfly Spread strategy requires adaptability to varying market conditions. Consider the following adjustments:

9.2.1 Expanding or Contracting Wings

- Adjust the width of the butterfly by selecting strike prices further apart for a wider spread or closer together for a narrower spread, depending on your market outlook.

9.2.2 Directional Bias Adjustments

- Introduce a directional bias by adjusting the placement of the central strike price based on your expectation of the underlying asset's movement.

9.2.3 Dynamic Management

- Monitor the trade as it progresses and adjust the strategy based on changing market conditions, such as increased or decreased volatility.

9.3 Risk Management: Key Considerations

Risk management is paramount in options trading, and the Butterfly Spread strategy is no exception. Consider the following key risk management considerations:

9.3.1 Defined Risk and Maximum Loss

- The Butterfly Spread inherently has a defined risk, limited to the initial net debit paid to establish the position.

9.3.2 Breakeven Points

- Be aware of the breakeven points, where the underlying asset's price at expiration results in neither a profit nor a loss.

9.3.3 Implied Volatility Impact

- Monitor implied volatility, as changes in volatility can impact the value of the options within the butterfly spread.

9.4 Profit Potential: Unlocking Gains in Low Volatility

Understanding the profit potential of a Butterfly Spread is essential for informed decision-making. Let's explore how profit is realized in this strategy:

9.4.1 Maximum Profit at Expiration

- The maximum profit occurs if the underlying asset closes at the central strike price at expiration. This results in the long options expiring in-the-money and the short options expiring worthless.

9.4.2 Gradual Profit Increase

- Profits increase gradually as the underlying asset's price approaches the central strike price, providing flexibility in managing the trade.

9.4.3 Limited Losses and Risk-Reward Ratio

- The risk-reward ratio is favorable, with limited losses and the potential for a significant gain relative to the initial net debit.

9.5 Case Studies: Navigating Butterfly Spread Trades

To enhance your understanding, let's delve into case studies that illustrate the implementation, management, and potential outcomes of Butterfly Spread trades in different market conditions:

9.5.1 Case Study 1: Successful Butterfly Spread in Low Volatility

- Analyze a case study where a Butterfly Spread thrives in a low-volatility environment, showcasing the strategy's effectiveness in such market conditions.

9.5.2 Case Study 2: Adjusting Wings in Response to Market Dynamics

- Explore a case study where the trader adjusts the width of the butterfly's wings in response to changing market dynamics, demonstrating adaptability.

9.6 Tips for Success: Enhancing Your Butterfly Spread Strategy

As you navigate the Butterfly Spread strategy, consider the following tips to optimize your approach:

9.6.1 Timely Adjustments

- Make timely adjustments based on changing market conditions to align the strategy with your evolving outlook.

9.6.2 Diversification

- Incorporate Butterfly Spreads as part of a diversified options trading portfolio to balance risk and return.

CHAPTER 10

RATIO SPREAD STRATEGY: LEVERAGING RISK AND REWARD

In this chapter, we'll explore how to implement Ratio Spreads, select the right ratio for specific market expectations, and discuss dynamic adjustments to optimize the strategy's performance.

10.1 The Ratio Spread Strategy: An Overview

The Ratio Spread strategy is a sophisticated options trading strategy that involves an unequal number of long and short options contracts. It is designed to achieve an asymmetric risk-reward profile, making it particularly suitable for traders with a directional bias. Let's break down the key components of the Ratio Spread:

10.1.1 Selecting Strike Prices

- Choose strike prices for the long and short options based on your market outlook. The strike prices determine the directional bias of the strategy.

10.1.2 Ratio of Long to Short Options

- The ratio refers to the unequal number of long and short options. For example, a 2:1 ratio means you buy two options and sell one.

10.1.3 Asymmetric Risk-Reward Profile

- The strategy aims to provide a favorable risk-reward ratio, allowing for potential gains in one direction while limiting losses in the other.

10.2 Implementing Ratio Spreads: Executing Asymmetric Trades

Successfully implementing Ratio Spreads requires a strategic approach to match your market expectations. Consider the following steps:

10.2.1 Directional Bias

- Determine your directional bias based on market analysis. Are you bullish, bearish, or neutral?

10.2.2 Strike Price Selection

- Choose strike prices that align with your directional bias. The distance between strike prices influences the risk-reward profile.

10.2.3 Ratio Determination

- Decide on the ratio of long to short options. Common ratios include 2:1, 3:2, or any other combination that fits your risk tolerance and outlook.

10.3 Selecting the Right Ratio: Tailoring to Market Expectations

The success of the Ratio Spread strategy hinges on selecting the right ratio that aligns with your specific market expectations. Let's explore considerations for choosing an appropriate ratio:

10.3.1 Neutral Outlook (1:1 Ratio)

- A 1:1 ratio is suitable for a neutral market outlook, where you expect the underlying asset to remain within a certain range.

10.3.2 Bullish Outlook (2:1 or 3:1 Ratio)

- For a bullish outlook, consider a higher ratio of long to short options (2:1 or 3:1), allowing for potential gains on an upward price movement.

10.3.3 Bearish Outlook (1:2 or 1:3 Ratio)

- Conversely, for a bearish outlook, opt for a higher ratio of short to long options (1:2 or 1:3), providing potential gains on a downward price movement.

10.4 Dynamic Adjustments: Fine-tuning the Strategy

To optimize the performance of Ratio Spreads, dynamic adjustments are often necessary to respond to changing market conditions. Consider the following approaches:

10.4.1 Rolling Options

- If the market moves against your position, consider rolling the options to a later expiration date or adjusting strike prices to manage risk.

10.4.2 Closing Positions

- If a substantial portion of the potential profit is realized, or the market conditions no longer support the original outlook, consider closing the position to secure gains.

10.4.3 Adding or Removing Options

- Depending on market developments, you may choose to add or remove options to modify the risk-reward profile of the strategy.

10.5 Case Studies: Navigating Ratio Spread Trades

To deepen your understanding, let's explore case studies that illustrate the implementation, management, and potential outcomes of Ratio Spread trades in different market scenarios:

10.5.1 Case Study 1: Successful Bullish Ratio Spread

- Analyze a case study where a trader implements a bullish Ratio Spread with a 2:1 ratio, capitalizing on a favorable market move.

10.5.2 Case Study 2: Adjusting a Neutral Ratio Spread

- Explore a case study where a trader dynamically adjusts a neutral Ratio Spread to respond to changing market conditions, showcasing adaptability.

10.6 Tips for Success: Enhancing Your Ratio Spread Strategy

As you venture into Ratio Spreads, consider the following tips to optimize your approach:

10.6.1 Regular Monitoring

- Regularly monitor your Ratio Spread positions to assess their alignment with market conditions and adjust as needed.

10.6.2 Scenario Planning

- Conduct scenario planning to anticipate potential market movements and adjust the ratio accordingly.

CONCLUSION

CRAFTING YOUR OPTIONS TRADING JOURNEY

Congratulations on completing this comprehensive guide to options trading strategies! You've embarked on a journey that delves into the intricacies of various options trading approaches, from foundational concepts to specialized strategies tailored for different market conditions. As you conclude this exploration, it's essential to reflect on the key takeaways and consider how to craft your unique path in the world of options trading.

1. Understanding the Foundations

At the beginning of your journey, you gained a solid understanding of the foundational concepts of options trading. You explored the basics of calls and puts, option pricing, and the Greeks. This knowledge forms the bedrock upon which you can build more advanced strategies.

2. Navigating Market Directions

Chapters on Long Call and Long Put strategies equipped you with the tools to navigate bullish and bearish market expectations. Whether you're looking to capitalize on upward price movements or profit from declines, these strategies provided you with insights into risk management and selecting the right strike prices and expiration dates.

3. Income Generation Strategies

Covered Calls and Credit Spreads emerged as powerful strategies for income generation. These chapters introduced you to the concept of writing options to collect premiums and balance risk and return. The covered call strategy allowed you to generate income with a safety net, while the credit spread strategy capitalized on time decay.

4. Risk Mitigation Strategies

Protective Puts and the Butterfly Spread strategy provided you with tools to safeguard your investments and capitalize on low volatility. These strategies allowed you to hedge against downside risk in a bearish market and leverage asymmetric risk-reward profiles in low volatility environments.

5. Profiting from Volatility

The Long Straddle strategy emerged as a key player in profiting from market volatility. By simultaneously buying call and put options, you gained insights into calculating breakeven points, potential gains, and adjusting the strategy for changing market conditions.

6. Crafting Directional Strategies

The Iron Condor strategy offered a nuanced approach for navigating sideways markets, showcasing the importance of constructing spreads to create profit zones and effectively manage risk in range-bound environments.

7. Leveraging Asymmetric Risk-Reward Profiles

The Ratio Spread strategy provided you with a specialized tool for leveraging asymmetric risk-reward profiles. By understanding how to implement ratios based on your directional bias, you gained insights into dynamic adjustments to optimize performance.

Crafting Your Unique Path

As you conclude this guide, it's important to recognize that crafting your options trading journey is a personalized endeavor. Consider your risk tolerance, market outlook, and investment goals. Options trading provides a diverse set of tools, and your success will hinge on your ability to adapt these strategies to your unique circumstances.

Key Considerations as You Craft Your Path:

1. **Risk Management:** Prioritize risk management in every strategy you implement. Define your risk tolerance and be disciplined in adhering to it.

2. **Adaptability:** Markets evolve, and successful options traders are adaptable. Regularly reassess your positions, adjust strategies based on changing market conditions, and stay informed about economic events that may impact your trades.

3. **Diversification:** Diversify your options trading portfolio to spread risk across different assets and strategies. This approach can help you navigate various market conditions more effectively.

4. **Continuous Learning:** The world of options trading is dynamic. Stay informed about market trends, new strategies, and evolving economic landscapes. Continuous learning is key to staying ahead in this ever-changing environment.

APPENDIX

ADVANCED CONCEPTS AND STRATEGIES

In this appendix, we will delve into advanced concepts and strategies that go beyond the foundational knowledge covered in the main guide. These advanced options strategies often involve a higher level of complexity and may require a more sophisticated understanding of market dynamics. Additionally, we will explore how options can be used in conjunction with other financial instruments and discuss risk management techniques tailored for advanced traders.

A.1 Advanced Options Strategies

A.1.1 Calendar Spreads (Time Spreads)

Calendar spreads involve the simultaneous purchase and sale of options with different expiration dates but the same strike prices. This strategy aims to capitalize on differences in implied volatility between short-term and long-term options. Learn how to construct and manage calendar spreads to take advantage of time decay differentials.

A.1.2 Ratio Diagonal Spreads

Ratio diagonal spreads combine elements of both ratio spreads and diagonal spreads. This advanced strategy incorporates different strike prices, expiration dates, and the ratio of long to short options. Explore how to implement and adjust ratio diagonal spreads for enhanced flexibility and risk management.

A.1.3 Iron Butterfly and Iron Condor Variations

Building on the foundational concepts of iron condors and iron butterflies, delve into variations of these strategies that involve different strike prices, wider spreads, or additional options. Understand how to tailor these strategies to specific market conditions and risk preferences.

A.1.4 Synthetic Options Positions

Synthetic options positions involve creating positions that mimic the risk and reward profile of standard options positions using a combination of other options and/or the underlying asset. Learn how to construct synthetic long calls, synthetic short puts, and other synthetic positions to achieve specific market exposures.

A.2 Using Options in Conjunction with Other Financial Instruments

A.2.1 Options and Stocks

Explore advanced techniques for combining options with stock positions to create more complex trading strategies. Learn how covered call writing, protective puts, and collars can be optimized to enhance risk management and returns when holding stock positions.

A.2.2 Options and Futures

Discover how options can be used in conjunction with futures contracts to create dynamic strategies. Explore the concept of options on futures and understand how these strategies can be employed for hedging, speculation, or income generation.

A.2.3 Options and ETFs

Understand how options can be effectively utilized with exchange-traded funds (ETFs) to create diverse and customizable investment strategies. Learn about leveraging options to enhance returns and manage risk in ETF portfolios.

A.3 Risk Management Techniques for Advanced Traders

A.3.1 Volatility Hedging

Delve into advanced techniques for hedging against volatility risk. Explore the use of options to create volatility hedges and understand how implied and historical volatility can be factored into risk management strategies.

A.3.2 Tail Risk Hedging

Tail risk hedging involves strategies designed to protect against extreme market events or "tail" events. Learn about tail risk hedging using options and other financial instruments to mitigate the impact of unforeseen market shocks.

A.3.3 Portfolio Margin and Advanced Risk Models

Explore the concept of portfolio margin, a risk-based margining system that allows traders to utilize leverage more efficiently. Understand how advanced risk models and quantitative analysis can be employed to optimize portfolio risk and return.

A.4 Conclusion of the Advanced Concepts Appendix

This appendix has provided a glimpse into the world of advanced options concepts and strategies. As you explore these advanced topics, keep in mind that each strategy carries its own risks and requires careful consideration. It is advisable to thoroughly understand the mechanics of each strategy and, if necessary, seek the guidance of financial professionals or advisors with expertise in advanced options trading.

Options trading at an advanced level involves a higher degree of complexity and risk. As you navigate this terrain, continuous learning, disciplined risk management, and a thorough understanding of market dynamics will be your allies. May your exploration of advanced options concepts contribute to your growth as a knowledgeable and strategic trader.

GLOSSARY

- **Call Option**: A financial contract giving the buyer the right, but not the obligation, to purchase an underlying asset at a predetermined price within a specified time frame.

- **Put Option**: A financial contract giving the buyer the right, but not the obligation, to sell an underlying asset at a predetermined price within a specified time frame.

- **Strike Price**: The price at which the underlying asset can be bought or sold, as specified in the options contract.

- **Expiration Date**: The date on which an options contract expires and becomes invalid.

- **Premium**: The price paid by the options buyer to the options seller for the rights conveyed by the options contract.

- **In-the-Money (ITM)**: A term used to describe options contracts that have intrinsic value. For call options, it means the stock price is above the strike price; for put options, it means the stock price is below the strike price.

- **At-the-Money (ATM)**: A term used to describe options contracts where the stock price is equal to the strike price.

- **Out-of-the-Money (OTM)**: A term used to describe options contracts that currently have no intrinsic value. For call options, it means the stock price is below the strike price; for put options, it means the stock price is above the strike price.

- **Delta**: A measure of how much an option's price is likely to change in response to a one-point change in the price of the underlying asset.

- **Gamma**: A measure of how much an option's delta is likely to change in response to a one-point change in the price of the underlying asset.

- **Theta**: A measure of how much the price of an option decreases as time passes, known as time decay.

- **Vega**: A measure of the sensitivity of an option's price to changes in volatility.

- **Implied Volatility (IV)**: The market's expectation of how much an underlying asset's price will fluctuate, as implied by options prices.

- **Long Call Strategy**: An options trading strategy where an investor buys call options to profit from an anticipated increase in the price of the underlying asset.

- **Long Put Strategy**: An options trading strategy where an investor buys put options to profit from an anticipated decrease in the price of the underlying asset.

- **Covered Call Strategy**: A strategy where an investor holds a long position in an asset and sells call options on that asset to generate income.

- **Protective Put Strategy**: A strategy where an investor purchases a put option to protect an existing long position in an asset from potential downside risk.

- **Long Straddle Strategy**: An options strategy where an investor simultaneously buys a call option and a put option with the same strike price and expiration date, anticipating a significant price movement.

- **Credit Spread Strategy**: A strategy where an investor sells one option and buys another option with the same expiration date but a different strike price, aiming to collect a net premium.

- **Iron Condor Strategy**: An options trading strategy that involves the simultaneous sale of a put spread and a call spread with the same expiration date but different strike prices.

- **Butterfly Spread Strategy**: An options strategy that involves using three strike prices to create a position consisting of both calls and puts for the same expiration date, aiming for a low-cost, low-risk position.

- **Ratio Spread Strategy**: An options strategy where the number of options bought or sold is unequal, creating an asymmetric risk-reward profile.

RESOURCES

- **Books:**
  - "Options, Futures, and Other Derivatives" by John C. Hull
  - "Option Volatility and Pricing" by Sheldon Natenberg
  - "The Intelligent Option Investor" by Erik Kobayashi-Solomon
- **Online Courses:**
  - Coursera - Options Trading Strategies
  - Udemy - Options Trading for Rookies: Make & Manage Profitable Trades
- **Websites:**
  - Investopedia Options Trading Section

- Options Industry Council (OIC)

- **Trading Platforms and Tools:**

  - Thinkorswim (by TD Ameritrade)

  - Interactive Brokers

  - OptionVue

Remember to conduct thorough research and practice with virtual accounts before engaging in live options trading. The world of options trading is dynamic, and ongoing education is essential for success. Happy learning and trading!

Manufactured by Amazon.ca
Acheson, AB

12361929R00046